MATERIALS

Anna Claybourne

Illustrated by Chrissy Barnard

WAYLAND
www.waylandbooks.co.uk

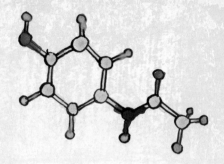

First published in 2014 by Wayland

Wayland
338 Euston Road
London NW1 3BH

Wayland Australia
Level 17/207 Kent Street
Sydney, NSW 2000

Series editor: Victoria Brooker
Series designer: Lisa Peacock

A CIP catalogue record for this book is available
from the British Library.
Dewey number: 620.1'1–dc23

ISBN: 978 0 7502 8278 9
Ebook ISBN: 978 0 7502 8834 7

10 9 8 7 6 5 4 3 2 1

Printed in China

Wayland is a division of Hachette Children's Books,
an Hachette UK Company
www.hachette.co.uk

Contents

Glossary 30

What are materials? 4

What is matter? 6

Index 32

Types of materials 8

Where materials come from 10

Materials

States of matter 12

Changes of state 14

Elements 16

Compounds 18

Using materials 28

Mixtures 20

Chemical reactions 22

Properties of materials 26

Reversible and non-reversible changes 24

What are materials?

Wherever you are, whatever you're doing, you're surrounded by stuff. It could be sofas, carpets, a tablet and a TV – or a classroom full of desks, pencils and books. Or if you're outside, it could be trees, grass, rocks or a sandy beach. You yourself, and your clothes, are also made of this 'stuff', which scientists call matter.

Everything around you that takes up space is made of matter. Water and other liquids are made of matter too, and so is the air we breathe. There are many different types of matter, making up all the different things around us – such as wood, plastic, water, iron, brick, oxygen, wool and paper.

These different types of matter are called materials. Some are natural materials, which occur naturally in the world around us, and some are artificial, and are made by humans. Materials have different properties, meaning the ways they behave and the things they can do.

Changing materials

Materials are found in three states, called the states of matter: solids, liquids and gases. Changes in temperature can cause a material to change from one to the other. For example, water is liquid at room temperature, but can freeze into ice, a solid, if it gets cold enough.

Materials can also change when they rearrange and combine in different ways to make new materials. This is called a chemical reaction.

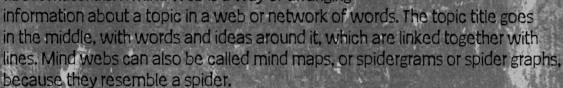

What is a mind web?

This book uses mind webs to show the basic facts about materials. A mind web is a way of arranging information about a topic in a web or network of words. The topic title goes in the middle, with words and ideas around it, which are linked together with lines. Mind webs can also be called mind maps, or spidergrams or spider graphs, because they resemble a spider.

A mind web is a great way to see everything about a topic at a glance, making it easier to remind yourself of all the facts. Mind webs can also have little pictures in them, to make things easier to remember.

This mini mind web shows you the main topics to do with materials. You will find more detailed mind webs about each of them in the rest of this book.

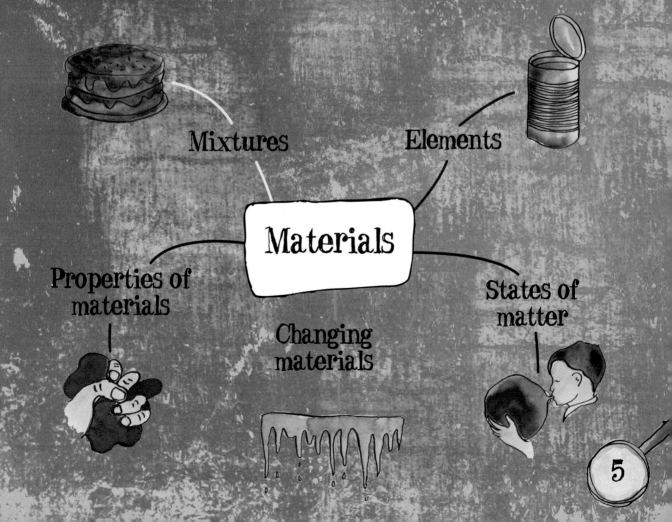

Mixtures

Elements

Materials

Properties of materials

Changing materials

States of matter

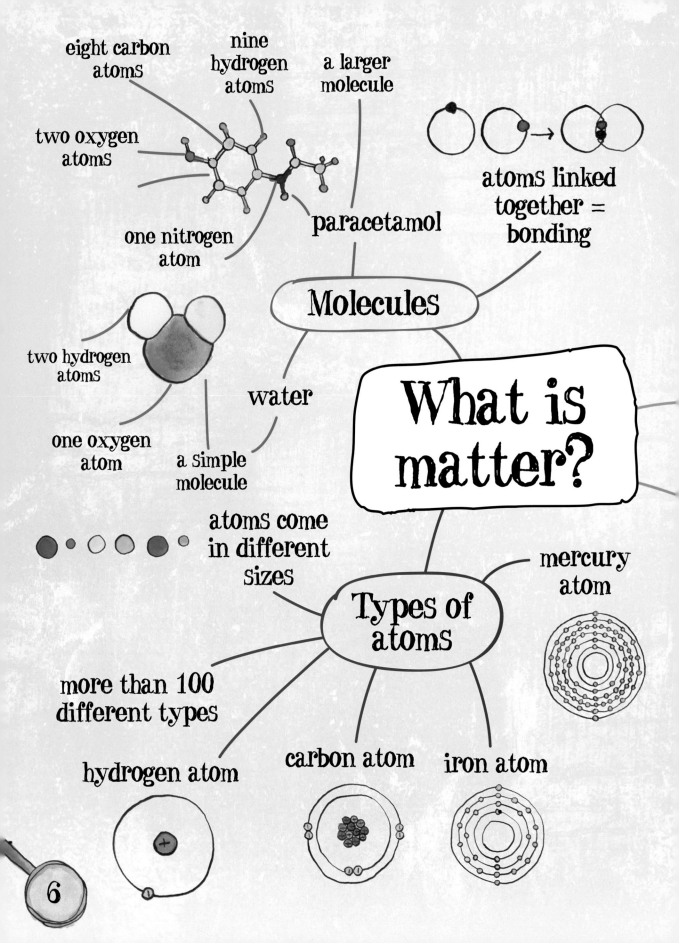

eight carbon atoms

nine hydrogen atoms

a larger molecule

two oxygen atoms

one nitrogen atom

paracetamol

atoms linked together = bonding

Molecules

two hydrogen atoms

one oxygen atom

water

a simple molecule

What is matter?

atoms come in different sizes

mercury atom

Types of atoms

more than 100 different types

hydrogen atom

carbon atom

iron atom

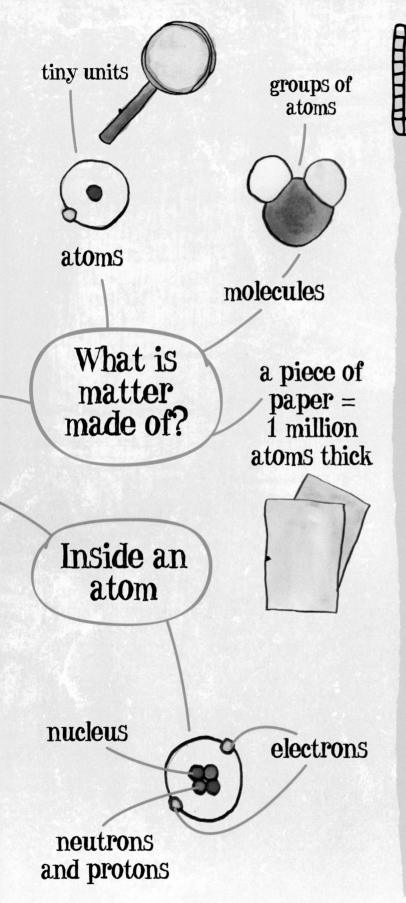

tiny units

groups of
atoms

atoms

molecules

What is
matter
made of?

a piece of
paper =
1 million
atoms thick

Inside an
atom

nucleus

electrons

neutrons
and protons

Although there are many types of materials, they all work the same way. All matter, and all materials, are made up of tiny units called atoms. Atoms can be linked together to form more complex units, called molecules.

Atoms

A typical atom is so small that one page in this book is about 1 million atoms thick. Atoms are made up of even tinier parts, or particles, called protons, neutrons and electrons. There are more than 100 different types of atoms, of different sizes (though they are all still very small). Hydrogen atoms are the smallest, for example, while an iron atom is bigger and has more parts.

Molecules

A molecule is made of two or more linked or bonded atoms. Atoms bond by sharing some of their electrons, which holds them together. Some molecules are very simple. Others, such as those that make food and plastics, can be much bigger and more complex.

Types of materials

There are millions of different materials, but they can be divided into several basic types. The simplest kind are pure, basic materials called elements. Around 100 of these are found on our planet, the Earth, including gold, oxygen, carbon and silicon. Each different type of atom makes up its own particular element. So, for example, the element iron is made of only iron atoms.

Elements can join together to make compounds, made up of elements joined together. In a compound, the atoms are bonded together to form molecules of that substance. For example, table salt is a common compound. It is made of sodium atoms and chlorine atoms, which are bonded together to form sodium chloride molecules. A teaspoon of salt is made up of these molecules.

Many materials are mixtures of several elements and compounds. Air, steel, milk, and concrete are examples of mixtures. A mixture may contain elements or compounds or both, but they are not all bonded together.

iron atoms

iron

around 100 types found on Earth

not bonded together

pure basic materials

material made of mixed elements or compounds

Mixtures

granite

everyday examples

soil

blood

chocolate cake

cup of coffee

glass

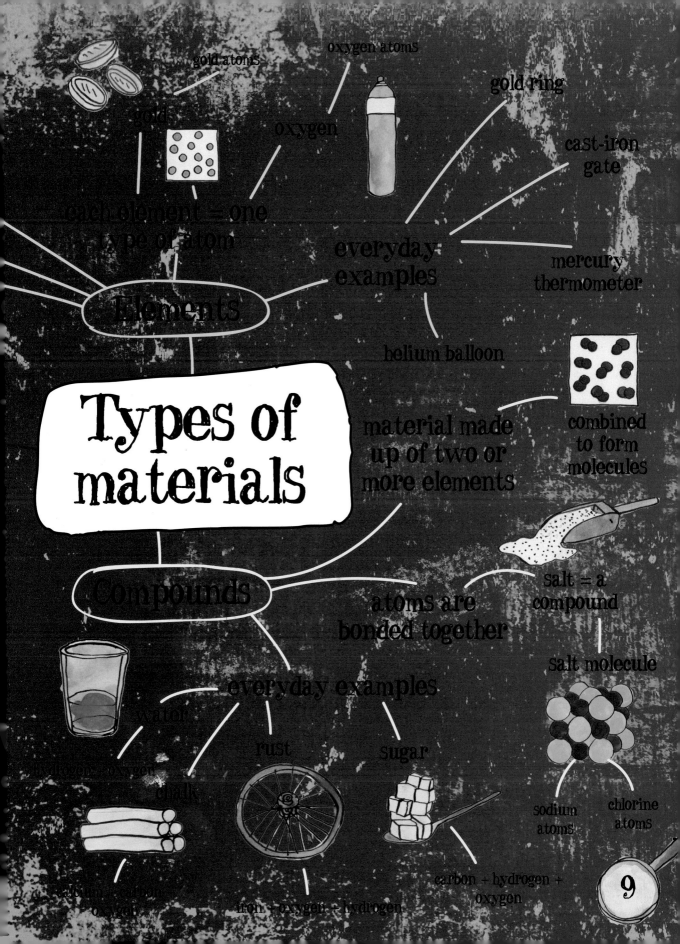

gold atoms

oxygen atoms

gold ring

gold

oxygen

cast-iron gate

each element = one type of atom

everyday examples

mercury thermometer

Elements

helium balloon

Types of materials

material made up of two or more elements

combined to form molecules

salt = a compound

Compounds

atoms are bonded together

salt molecule

water

everyday examples

sodium atoms

chlorine atoms

hydrogen + oxygen

chalk

rust

sugar

calcium + carbon + oxygen

iron + oxygen + hydrogen

carbon + hydrogen + oxygen

9

Where materials come from

The Earth itself is made of matter, and this is where we get all the materials that we use to make things. Some we collect and use as they are, like wood and stone. We can also process, mix and change naturally occurring materials to make new materials.

Natural materials

Many natural materials can come from the Earth itself. They include many types of rocks and minerals, oil and gas, and water. We also make use of animal materials, such as leather, wool and bone, and vegetable materials, which come from plants, such as wood, cotton and bamboo.

Artificial materials

Artificial materials are materials made by humans. Of course, to make them we have to use natural materials, but they are often changed completely to make something new. For example, a nylon raincoat is made from a type of plastic, which is made from chemicals extracted from oil found in the ground.

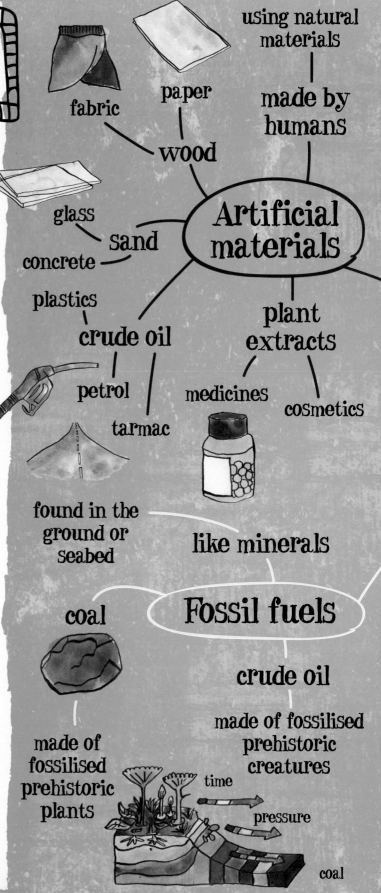

fabric

paper

using natural materials

made by humans

wood

glass

sand

Artificial materials

concrete

plastics

crude oil

plant extracts

petrol

medicines

cosmetics

tarmac

found in the ground or seabed

like minerals

coal

Fossil fuels

crude oil

made of fossilised prehistoric plants

made of fossilised prehistoric creatures

time

pressure

coal

Where materials come from

Animal
- yak — wool
- sheep — wool
- coral reefs — coral
- cow — leather
- abalone — shell
- honeybee — beeswax
- caterpillar — silk

Vegetable
- trees — wood
- cotton plant — cotton
- cork tree — cork
- rubber tree — rubber

Mineral
- silver — metals
- copper — metals
- precious stones
- sand
- clay
- stone — sandstone
- stone — marble

11

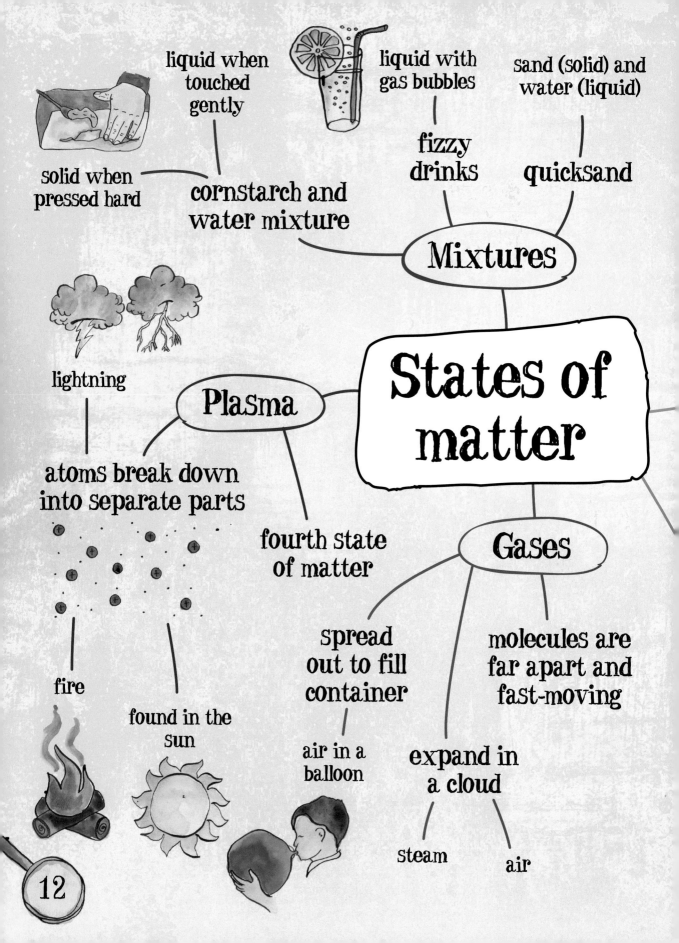

liquid when touched gently

solid when pressed hard

cornstarch and water mixture

liquid with gas bubbles

fizzy drinks

sand (solid) and water (liquid)

quicksand

Mixtures

States of matter

lightning

Plasma

atoms break down into separate parts

fourth state of matter

fire

found in the sun

Gases

spread out to fill container

molecules are far apart and fast-moving

air in a balloon

expand in a cloud

steam

air

States of matter

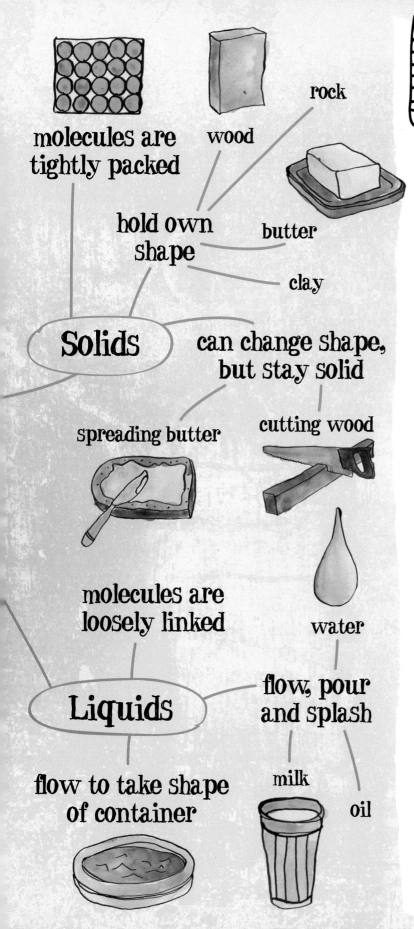

molecules are tightly packed

rock

wood

butter

hold own shape

clay

Solids

can change shape, but stay solid

spreading butter

cutting wood

water

molecules are loosely linked

flow, pour and splash

Liquids

milk

oil

flow to take shape of container

Most materials are either solids, liquids or gases. These are called the three states of matter.

Solids, like a plank of wood or a rock, tend to keep their shape. Solids can change shape if something happens to them, such as sawing wood, but they stay solid. In a solid, the molecules are tightly packed.

Liquids flow, splash and pour. If you put a liquid such as water into a container, it will flow around and take the shape of the container. In a liquid, the molecules are connected loosely, so they can flow and slip past each other.

Gases spread out to fill the space they are in. If you release gas into a room, it will spread out all over the room. The molecules in a gas are spaced far apart and zoom around at high speed.

Some materials contain mixtures of states of matter, or can behave in different ways in different situations. There is also a different state of matter, plasma, in which atoms are broken down. Fire is a form of plasma.

gas

solid carbon
dioxide

dry ice

gas canister

gas becomes
a liquid

pressure pushes
molecules together

Sublimation

Pressure

solid can change
directly into a gas

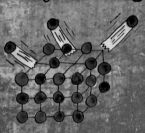

Changes of state

butter melts in pan

melting

Everyday examples

icicles thaw
and drip

evaporating

condensing

freezing

clothes dry on a
washing line

clouds form and
become rain

pond freezes
in winter

lava
hardening on
a volcano

pan boils dry

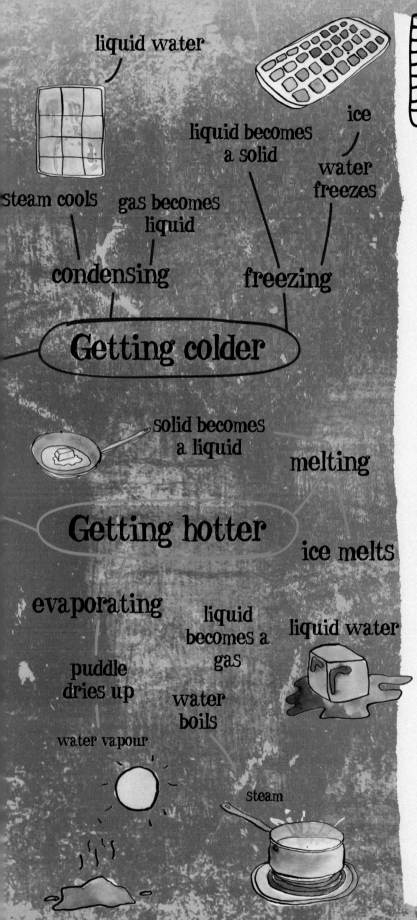

liquid water

ice

liquid becomes
a solid

water
freezes

steam cools

gas becomes
liquid

condensing

freezing

Getting colder

solid becomes
a liquid

melting

Getting hotter

ice melts

evaporating

liquid
becomes a
gas

liquid water

puddle
dries up

water
boils

water vapour

steam

A material can change from one state of matter to another, usually due to changes in temperature. For example, when water is below 0°C, it is a solid, ice. When it warms up to a higher temperature, it melts. Above 100°C, it boils and evaporates into a gas. Liquids can also evaporate more slowly at lower temperatures, like when a puddle dries in the sun. The same happens in reverse. As steam cools down, it condenses into liquid. The liquid water can then freeze into ice.

Adding energy

As a material heats up, its molecules get more energy and this makes them move more. The faster-moving molecules break away from each other more easily, turning a solid into a flowing liquid, or a liquid into a gas. It's also possible to change the state of a material using pressure. Cooking gas, for example, can be stored under high pressure in a container. This makes it into a liquid until it escapes from the container.

Elements

Elements are basic materials that form the building blocks of other materials. They include several everyday materials such as iron, tin and oxygen and precious materials such as gold and platinum. There are also many rare or little-known elements like dysprosium, whose name means 'hard to find', and curium, named after the scientist Marie Curie. Altogether, around 100 elements are found on the Earth. They are divided into three main types: metals, metalloids and non-metals.

One ingredient

Each element is made of only one single type of atom. So, for example, iron is made of iron atoms, gold is made of gold atoms and carbon is made of carbon atoms. Other materials are made from different types of atoms joined or mixed together, but elements are pure.

The Periodic Table

Scientists arrange the elements, according to their properties and the size of their atoms, in a large chart called the Periodic Table. Each element has its own number, called its atomic number, and its own letter symbol.

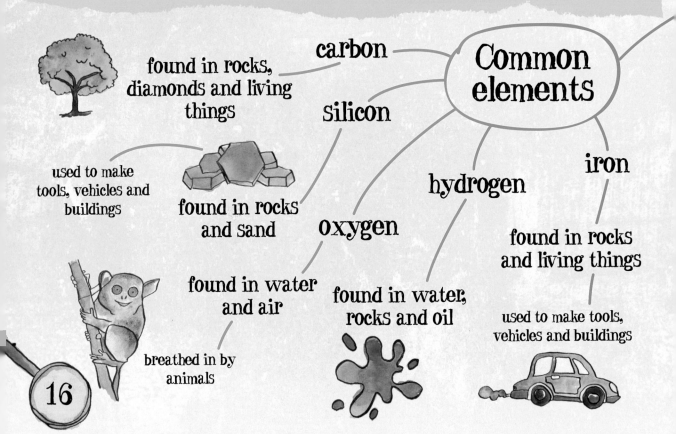

carbon — found in rocks, diamonds and living things

Common elements

silicon — found in rocks and sand

used to make tools, vehicles and buildings

oxygen — found in water and air

breathed in by animals

hydrogen — found in water, rocks and oil

iron — found in rocks and living things

used to make tools, vehicles and buildings

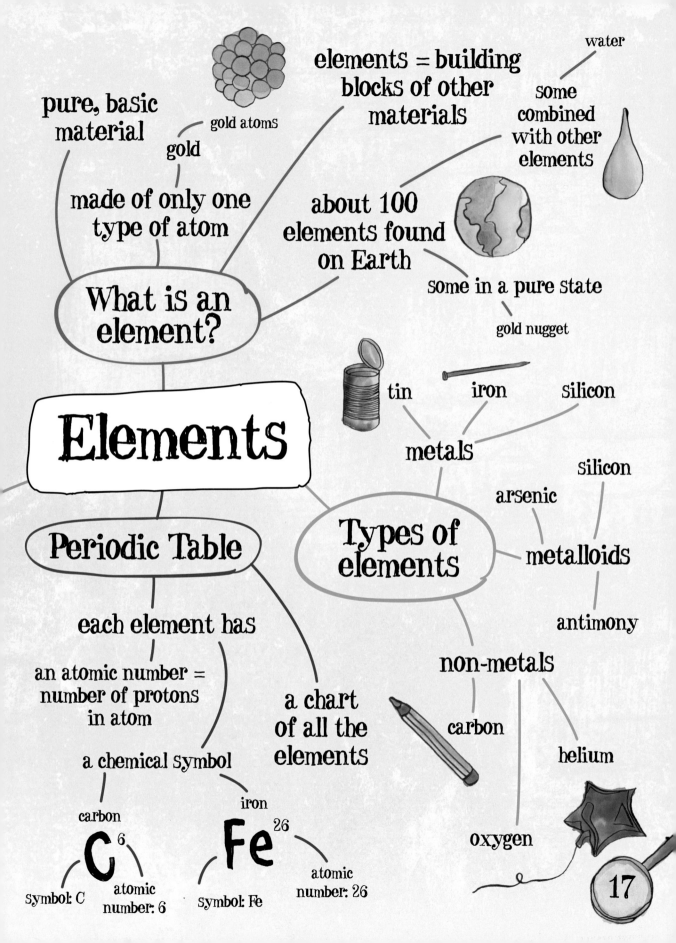

pure, basic material

gold atoms

gold

elements = building blocks of other materials

water

some combined with other elements

made of only one type of atom

about 100 elements found on Earth

What is an element?

some in a pure state

gold nugget

Elements

tin

iron

silicon

metals

silicon

arsenic

metalloids

Types of elements

antimony

Periodic Table

each element has

non-metals

an atomic number = number of protons in atom

a chart of all the elements

carbon

helium

a chemical symbol

carbon

C ^{6}

iron

Fe ^{26}

oxygen

symbol: C

atomic number: 6

symbol: Fe

atomic number: 26

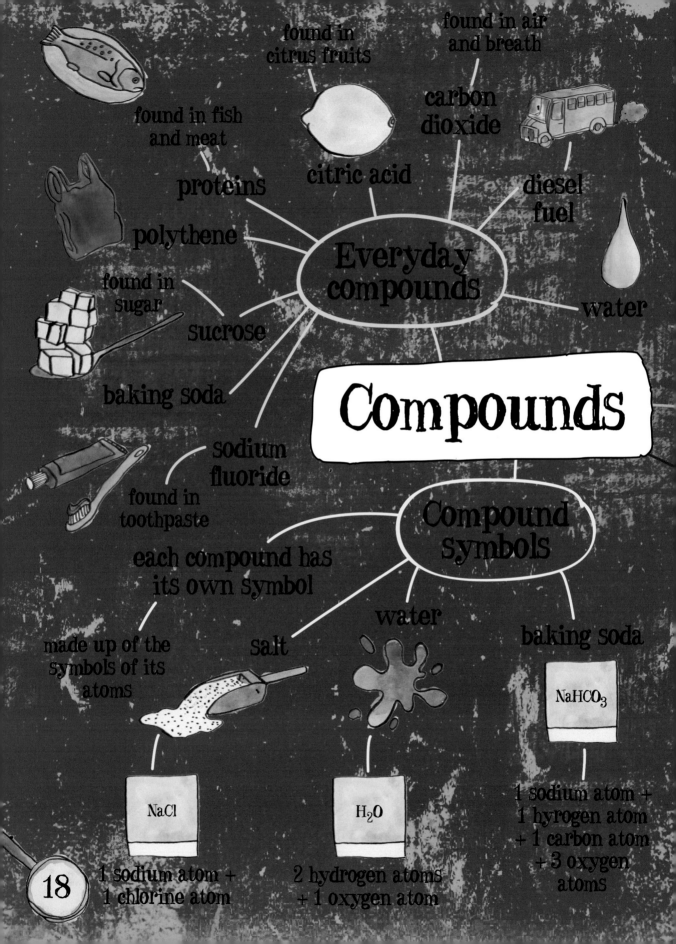

found in citrus fruits

found in air and breath

carbon dioxide

found in fish and meat

citric acid

proteins

diesel fuel

polythene

Everyday compounds

found in sugar

water

sucrose

Compounds

baking soda

sodium fluoride

Compound Symbols

found in toothpaste

each compound has its own symbol

water

made up of the symbols of its atoms

salt

baking soda

$NaHCO_3$

$NaCl$

H_2O

1 sodium atom + 1 hyrogen atom + 1 carbon atom + 3 oxygen atoms

1 sodium atom + 1 chlorine atom

2 hydrogen atoms + 1 oxygen atom

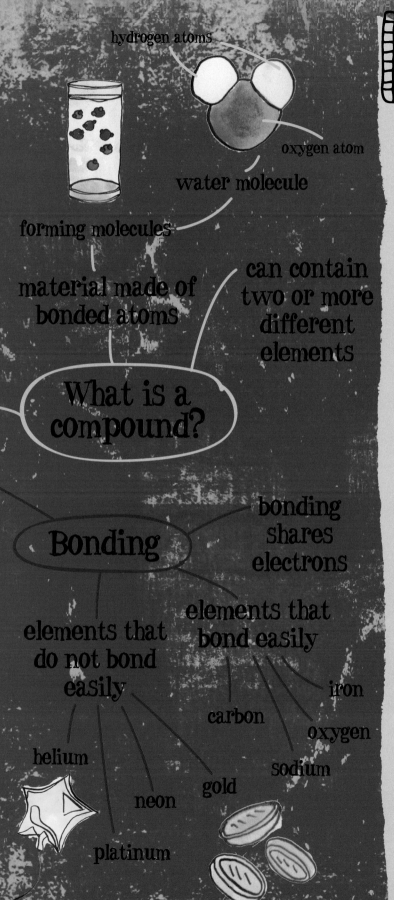

hydrogen atoms

oxygen atom

water molecule

forming molecules

material made of bonded atoms

can contain two or more different elements

What is a compound?

bonding shares electrons

Bonding

elements that do not bond easily

elements that bond easily

iron

carbon

oxygen

sodium

helium

gold

neon

platinum

Compounds

A compound is a material made of two or more different elements joined together. The atoms of the elements are linked, or bonded, to make molecules of that compound. This means that the compound is the same all the way through.

Common compounds include water, salt, rust and limestone. Acids, found in lemon juice and vinegar, are a type of compound. So are plastics such as nylon and polythene. Foods, such as bread, sugar and butter, contain many compounds too, and so do our own bodies.

How atoms bond

Atoms have a nucleus in the middle, surrounded by a cloud of electrons. When atoms bond, they join together in a way that lets them share their electrons. Some atoms bond easily, because they have 'gaps' in their groups of electrons. They naturally try to fill the gaps by bonding onto other atoms. For example, iron, oxygen and carbon are like this. Other atoms, such as gold, do not bond easily. This is why gold is often found as pure nuggets.

Mixtures

In a mixture, different materials are mixed together, but their atoms are not bonded. There are thousands of mixtures all around us, such as air, soil, seawater, many types of rock, shower gel, milk, bread or a sweater made of mixed fibres. We often make mixtures for particular purposes, such as steel, a very strong mixture of iron and carbon used in buildings and tools.

Types of mixtures

There are various types of mixtures. An alloy is a mixture of two metals, or a metal and another element, blended together. A suspension is a liquid or gas with tiny solid particles mixed into it, and an emulsion is a liquid containing tiny drops of another liquid. In a solution, the molecules of one material, such as salt, are dissolved or spread out into another, such as water.

Separating mixtures

It's possible to separate some mixtures back into their original materials. For example, if you heat water with salt dissolved in it, the water will evaporate, leaving the salt behind.

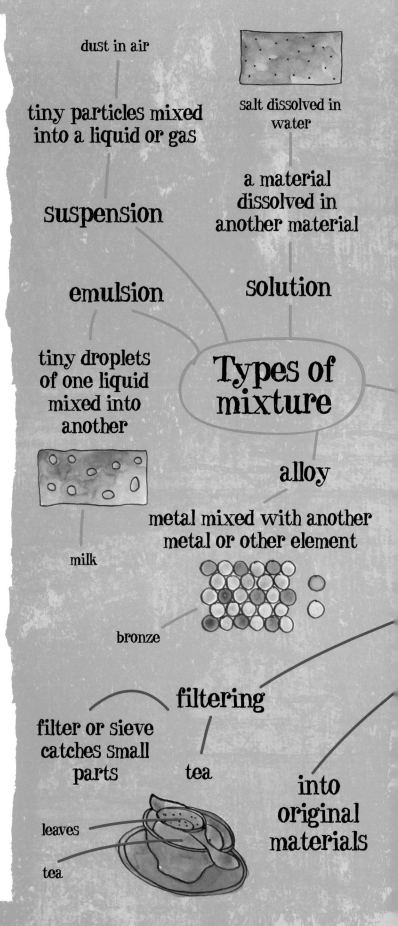

dust in air

tiny particles mixed into a liquid or gas

salt dissolved in water

suspension

a material dissolved in another material

emulsion

solution

tiny droplets of one liquid mixed into another

Types of mixture

alloy

metal mixed with another metal or other element

milk

bronze

filtering

filter or sieve catches small parts

tea

into original materials

leaves

tea

elements or compounds mixed together

atoms and molecules are not all bonded

brass

honey

smooth and evenly mixed

homogenous mixtures

fruit salad

What is a mixture?

heterogenous mixtures

not smoothly mixed

gravel

Mixtures

soup

washing-up liquid

Separating mixtures

Everyday mixtures

glue

evaporation

nail polish

water

mayonnaise

blueberry muffin

salt

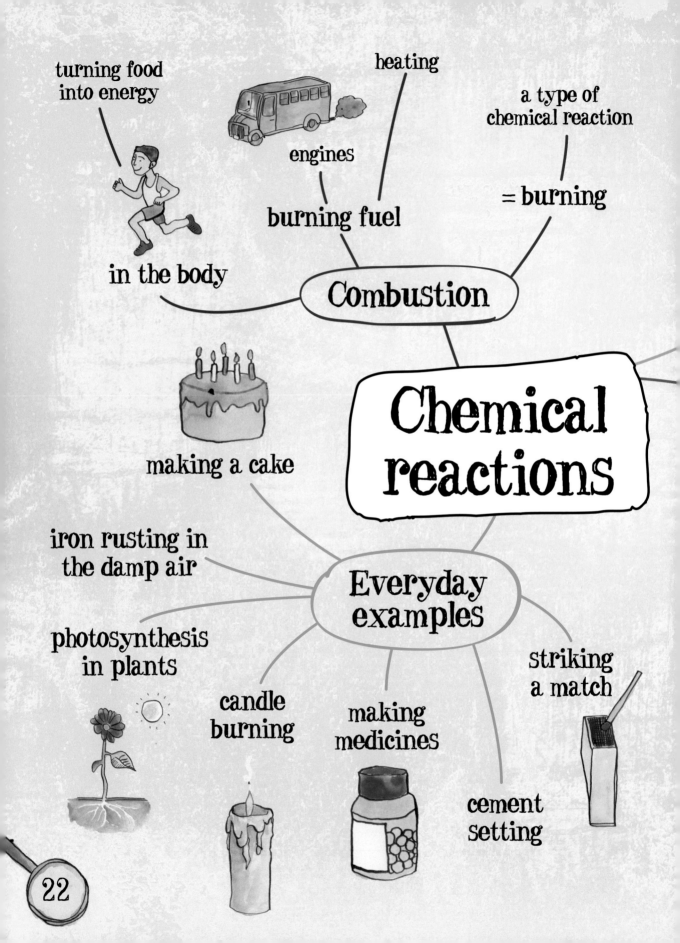

turning food
into energy

heating

a type of
chemical reaction

engines

= burning

burning fuel

in the body

Combustion

Chemical reactions

making a cake

iron rusting in
the damp air

Everyday
examples

photosynthesis
in plants

striking
a match

candle
burning

making
medicines

cement
setting

carbon dioxide CO_2 +
water H_2O + sodium
acetate NaC_2H3O_2

new materials form

vinegar HC_2H3O_2 + baking soda $NaHCO_3$

What is a chemical reaction?

materials combine and change

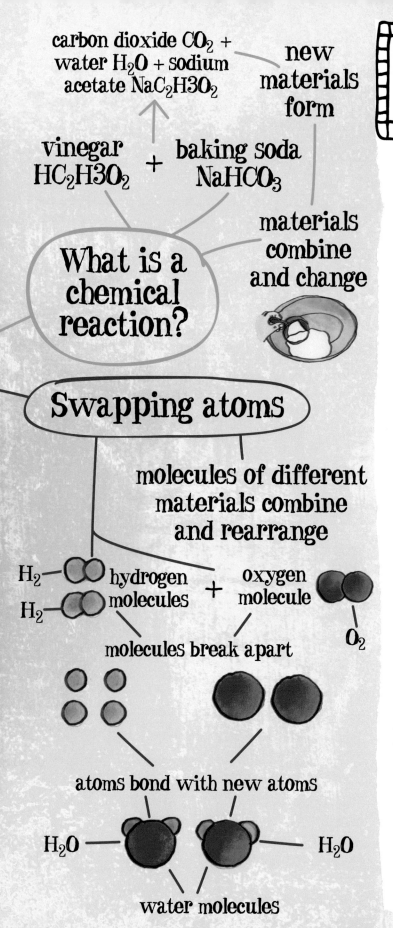

Swapping atoms

molecules of different materials combine and rearrange

H_2 hydrogen molecules + oxygen molecule
H_2

O_2

molecules break apart

atoms bond with new atoms

H_2O — — H_2O

water molecules

If you mix vinegar (liquid) with baking soda (solid), something happens! The mixture fizzes and froths and you get bubbles of gas. The gas is carbon dioxide, which is not part of either vinegar or baking soda. It has appeared because of a chemical reaction.

Swapping atoms
In a chemical reaction, the atoms in a material can break their bonds and rearrange themselves. You can put two or more materials in, and come out with completely different materials made from the same elements. Some chemical reactions also release heat – especially combustion, or burning, which is a type of chemical reaction.

Reactions everywhere
Chemical reactions are happening all the time. As well as being set up in chemistry labs, they happen in cooking, and are used to turn natural materials into artificial materials, such as medicines, paints or plastics.

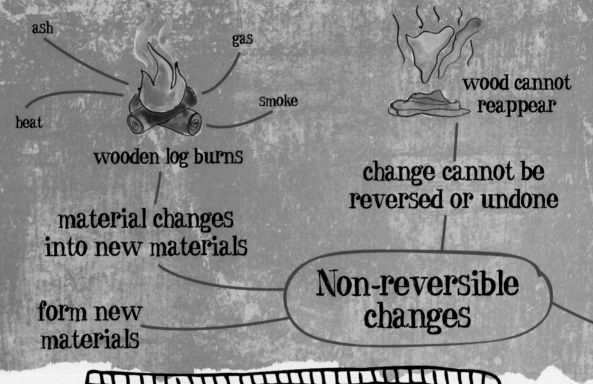

ash

gas

heat

smoke

wooden log burns

wood cannot reappear

material changes
into new materials

change cannot be
reversed or undone

form new
materials

Non-reversible changes

Reversible and non-reversible changes

The changes that happen to materials can be divided into reversible changes and non-reversible changes.

Reversible changes

A reversible change means a change that can be reversed, or undone – in other words, the material can change back to how it was before. One example is water freezing and melting. When the temperature drops below 0°C, the water in a pond will freeze into solid ice. But as the temperature warms up again, the ice turns back into liquid water. The change does not form new materials.

Non-reversible changes

A non-reversible change is a change that cannot be reversed or undone. As the material changes, new materials are formed and it cannot go back to how it was before. Burning and many types of chemical reaction are non-reversible changes. For example, when you burn a piece of wood, it changes into ash, heat and gases. The process cannot be reversed to make the same piece of wood again.

Reversible and non-reversible changes

Everyday examples

reversible

salt dissolves in water

water evaporates

salt left behind

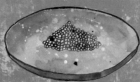

plastic picture beads

ironing melts beads

beads harden again when cool

non-reversible

cannot 'unset'

concrete sets hard

boiling an egg

egg turns solid

egg cools

Reversible changes

no new materials

material changes state or appearance

water freezes into ice

change can be reversed or undone

ice melts back into water

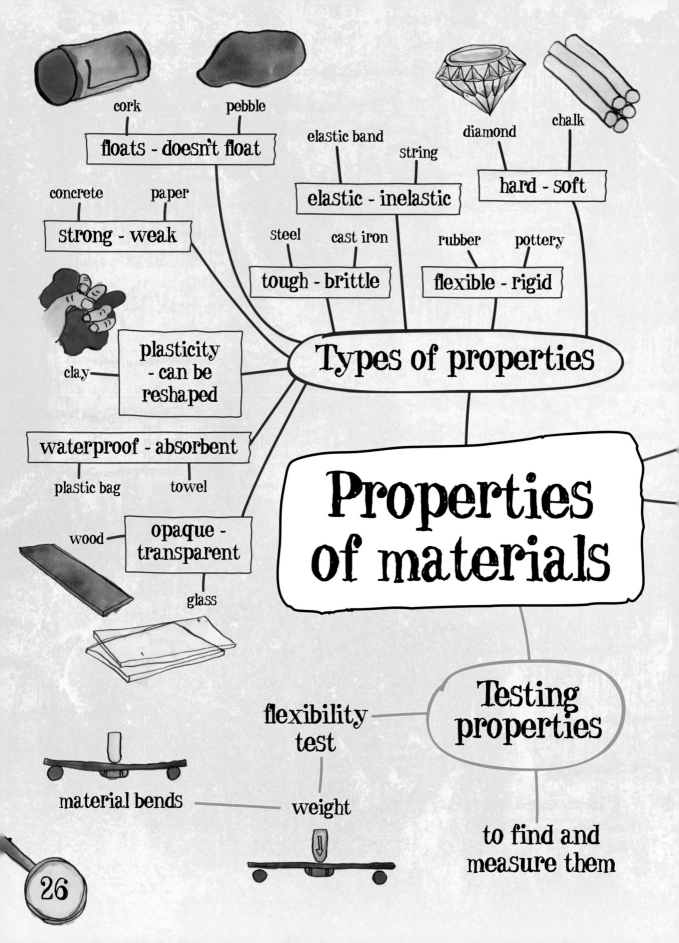

cork

pebble

floats - doesn't float

concrete   paper

elastic band

string

diamond

chalk

strong - weak

elastic - inelastic

hard - soft

steel   cast iron

rubber   pottery

tough - brittle

flexible - rigid

plasticity
- can be
reshaped

clay

Types of properties

waterproof - absorbent

Properties
of materials

plastic bag   towel

wood

opaque -
transparent

glass

Testing
properties

flexibility
test

material bends

weight

to find and
measure them

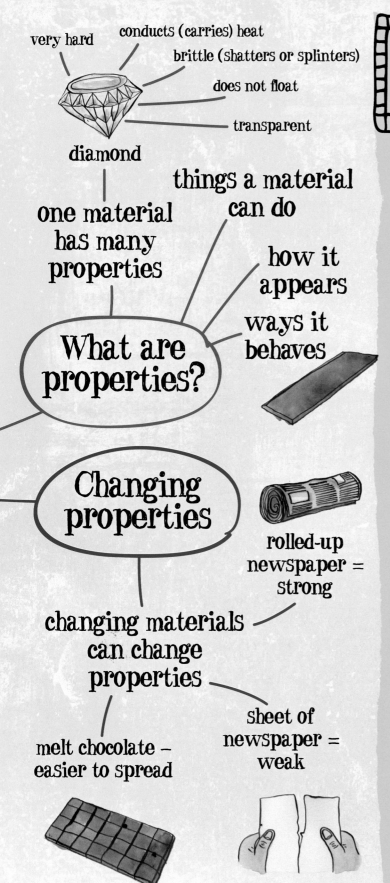

very hard

conducts (carries) heat

brittle (shatters or splinters)

does not float

transparent

diamond

things a material can do

one material has many properties

how it appears

ways it behaves

What are properties?

Changing properties

rolled-up newspaper = strong

changing materials can change properties

melt chocolate – easier to spread

sheet of newspaper = weak

Properties of materials

All materials have properties. A material's properties mean the things it can do, what it is like and the ways it behaves. For example, diamond is a material whose properties include being transparent (see-through) and very hard.

Types of properties
There are many different types of properties that materials can have. Here are a few of them:
- Hardness/softness – how difficult or easy it is to scratch
- Elasticity – how springy it is
- Density – how heavy it is for its size and whether it floats in water
- Plasticity – how easy it is to reshape
- Absorbency – how well it soaks up water

Testing properties
Scientists can test materials to measure their properties. For example, if someone invented a new material for building bridges, it would have to be tested for strength. One test would be to see how much pressure it would take to break a piece of the material.

Using materials

When it comes to using materials, their properties are very important. The jobs a material can do depend on its properties, so we have to pick the right materials for the right purpose.

Natural materials

Since ancient times, people have been using the best materials they could find for what they needed. Wood and bamboo are strong and easy to cut, so they were good for building houses. Stacking up stones made stronger walls and castles. Clay from the ground could be shaped into bowls that hardened in the sun. Humans also discovered how to get strong, flexible metals from the ground for making weapons and tools.

Making materials

Over time, we've found ways of improving materials to give them even more useful properties. For example, mixing other materials in with iron makes steel, which is stronger and rusts less. And we are still developing new materials, such as super-strong graphene.

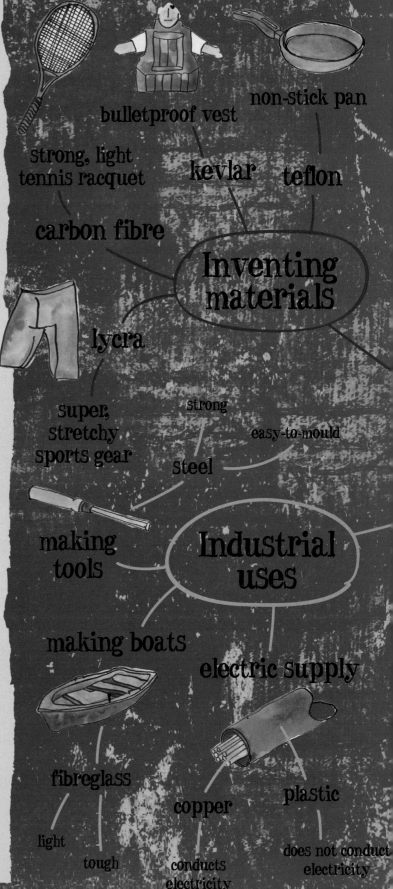

bulletproof vest

non-stick pan

strong, light tennis racquet

kevlar

teflon

carbon fibre

Inventing materials

lycra

super, stretchy sports gear

strong

easy-to-mould

steel

making tools

Industrial uses

making boats

electric supply

fibreglass

plastic

light

copper

tough

conducts electricity

does not conduct electricity

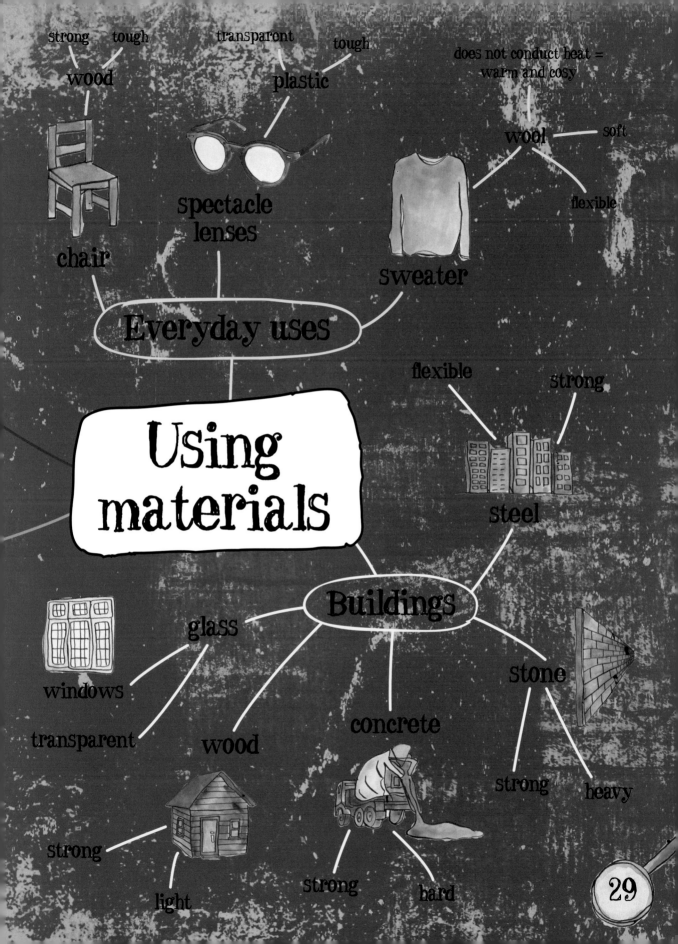

strong   tough

wood

transparent

tough

plastic

does not conduct heat =
warm and cosy

wool

soft

flexible

spectacle
lenses

chair

sweater

Everyday uses

flexible

strong

Using
materials

steel

Buildings

glass

windows

stone

transparent

wood

concrete

strong   heavy

strong

strong

light

strong

hard

29

Glossary

alloy A mixture of one metal with another metal or another element.

artificial materials Materials made by humans.

atomic number A number given to each element, based on the number of protons it has.

atoms The tiny units that materials are made up of.

bond A link between atoms that have joined together by sharing electrons.

carbon A very common element found in rocks and living things.

carbon dioxide A type of gas made up of carbon and oxygen.

chemical reaction A change that happens when materials combine and exchange atoms.

combustion A scientific name for burning.

compound A material made of different elements bonded together to form molecules.

condense To change from a gas to a liquid.

conduct To carry heat or electricity through a material.

dissolve To break apart into tiny bits and spread out through a liquid.

electrons Tiny particles that zoom around the outer part of an atom.

element A pure, basic material made up of only one type of atom.

emulsion A mixture made of tiny droplets of one liquid mixed into another liquid.

energy The power to do work or make things happen.

evaporate To change from a liquid to a gas.

gas A state of matter in which molecules are moving fast and are widely spread out.

liquid A state of matter in which molecules are loosely linked, that can flow and pour.

materials Types of matter.

matter The stuff that all the objects and materials around us are made of.

metalloid A type of element that is similar in some ways to a metal.

metals A group of elements that includes iron, gold and copper.

mixture A material made of a combination of elements or compounds that are not all bonded together.

molecules Units of matter made of atoms bonded together.

natural materials Materials found in the natural world.

neutrons Tiny particles found inside atoms.

non-reversible change A change that cannot be reversed or undone.

nucleus The middle part of an atom.

opaque Non-transparent and unable to let light through.

oxygen A very common element found in living things and as a gas in the air.

Periodic Table A large chart that lists all the known elements.

plasma A special state of matter in which electrons get separated from their atoms.

properties The things a material can do and the ways it behaves.

protons Tiny particles found inside atoms.

reversible change A change that can be reversed or undone.

solid A state of matter in which molecules are tightly packed, and that keeps its shape.

solution A mixture made of molecules of one material mixed into another.

states of matter The forms that matter can exist in, such as solid, liquid or gas.

suspension A liquid or gas with tiny particles of a solid mixed into it.

Index

alloy 20, 30
animals 10, 11, 16
artificial materials 4, 10
  23, 30
atomic number 16, 17, 30
atoms 6, 7, 13, 16, 18,
  19, 20, 23, 30

bonding 6, 7, 19, 23, 30

carbon 6, 8, 9, 16, 17, 19,
  20, 28, 30
carbon dioxide 18, 23, 30
chemical reactions 4,
  22–23, 24, 30
combustion 22, 23, 30
compounds 8, 9, 18–19,
  21, 30
condensation 15, 30
conduction 27, 28, 30

dissolving 20, 25, 30

electrons 7, 19, 30
elements 8, 9, 16–17,
  19, 20, 21, 23, 30
emulsion 20, 30
energy 15, 22, 30
evaporation 14, 15, 20, 21,
  25, 30

fossil fuels 10

gases 10, 12, 13, 14, 15,
  20, 23, 24, 30

hydrogen 6, 7, 9, 16, 18,
  19, 23

iron 6, 7, 8, 9, 16, 17, 19,
  20, 22, 28

liquids 12, 13, 14, 15, 20,
  23, 24, 30

matter 4, 6–7, 10, 12–13,
  30
metalloid 16, 17, 30
metals 11, 16, 17, 20,
  28, 30
minerals 10, 11
mixtures 8, 12, 20–21, 30
molecules 6, 7, 8, 9, 12, 13,
  14, 15, 19, 20, 21, 23, 31

natural materials 4, 10, 23,
  28, 31
neutrons 7, 31
non-reversible change 24,
  25, 31
nucleus 7, 19, 31

oxygen 6, 9, 16, 17, 18, 19,
  23, 31

Periodic Table 16, 17, 31
plasma 12, 13, 31
plants 10, 11
plastic 7, 10, 19, 23, 25,
  28, 29
pressure 10, 14, 15, 27
properties 4, 16, 26–27,
  28, 31
protons 7, 17, 31

reversible change 24, 25,
  31

solids 13, 14, 15, 20, 23,
  24, 25, 31
solutions 20, 31
states of matter 4, 12–16,
  31
sublimation 14
suspensions 20, 31

temperature 4, 15, 24

water 6, 15, 16, 17, 18, 19,
  20, 23, 24, 25